SAFETY AT HOME

Written by
Susan Kesselring

Illustrated by
Dan McGeehan

SAFETY FIRST

www.av2books.com

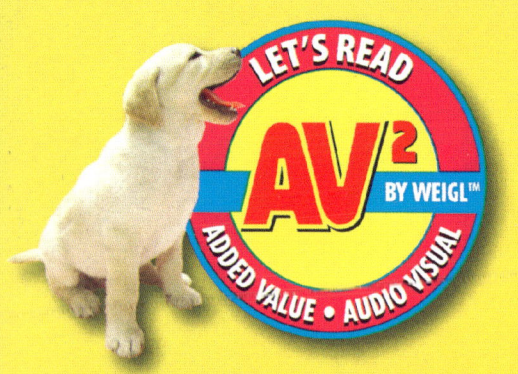

AV² provides enriched content that supplements and complements this book. Weigl's AV² books strive to create inspired learning and engage young minds in a total learning experience.

Your AV² Media Enhanced books come alive with...

Audio
Listen to sections of the book read aloud.

Video
Watch informative video clips.

Embedded Weblinks
Gain additional information for research.

Try This!
Complete activities and hands-on experiments.

Key Words
Study vocabulary, and complete a matching word activity.

Quizzes
Test your knowledge.

Slide Show
View images and captions, and prepare a presentation.

... and much, much more!

Go to www.av2books.com, and enter this book's unique code.

BOOK CODE

AVE76454

AV² by Weigl brings you media enhanced books that support active learning.

Published by AV² by Weigl
350 5th Avenue, 59th Floor New York, NY 10118
Website: www.av2books.com

Copyright ©2020 AV² by Weigl
All rights reserved. No part of this publication may be reproduced, stored in a retrieval system, or transmitted in any form or by any means, electronic, mechanical, photocopying, recording, or otherwise, without the prior written permission of the publisher.

Library of Congress Cataloging-in-Publication Data

Names: Kesselring, Susan, author.
Title: Safety at home / Susan Kesselring.
Other titles: Being safe at home
Description: New York, NY : AV² by Weigl, [2020] | Series: Safety first | Revised editon of: Being safe at home. | Audience: Grades K to 3.
Identifiers: LCCN 2018053395 (print) | LCCN 2018056481 (ebook) | ISBN 9781489699619 (Multi User Ebook) |
ISBN 9781489699626 (Single User Ebook) | ISBN 9781489699596 (hardcover : alk. paper) | ISBN 9781489699602 (softcover : alk. paper)
Subjects: LCSH: Home accidents--Prevention--Juvenile literature. | Safety education--Juvenile literature.
Classification: LCC TX150 (ebook) | LCC TX150 .K47 2020 (print) | DDC 363.13/7--dc23
LC record available at https://lccn.loc.gov/2018053395

Printed in the United States of America in Brainerd, Minnesota
1 2 3 4 5 6 7 8 9 0 22 21 20 19 18

112018
102918

Project Coordinator: Jared Siemens   Designer: Ana María Vidal

First published by The Child's World in 2011

SAFETY AT HOME

In this book, you will learn about

home safety,

what to do,

what not to do,

and much more!

What fun things do you do at home? Are you a block builder or a car racer? Do you dress up dolls or put puzzles together? Or do you like to make popcorn or grilled cheese sandwiches with your mom or dad?

Playing and cooking at home can be fun! You do have to be careful, though. Just remember to follow a few safety rules and you won't get hurt.

Hi! I'm Buzz B. Safe. Watch for me! I will show you how to be safe at home.

6

Cooking is a yummy way to have fun! But be careful with hot food. Always ask an adult to take the hot food out of a microwave or an oven for you.

It is easy to cut yourself with a sharp knife. Let your mom or dad chop the vegetables and slice the bread.

Even though you should not use a knife, you can still help out at dinnertime. Offer to wash the vegetables or set the table.

8

It's fun to move, skip, and dance in your home. You could trip or fall if you do not have a clear path. Pick up toys and keep other things off the stairs and floors. You don't want anyone else to fall, either.

Watch where you step in the bathroom or the kitchen. Water may have fallen on the floor. It could be slippery.

A rubber mat in the tub will help keep you from slipping.

10

Climbing things is a fun way to play. It is not very safe, though. Stay off tall furniture, drawers, and shelves. They could fall on you.

Window screens keep bugs out of your home. They are not very strong, though. They will not keep you from falling out. It's safest to play away from open windows.

Be careful around drapes and blinds. Their cords could twist around your neck and choke you.

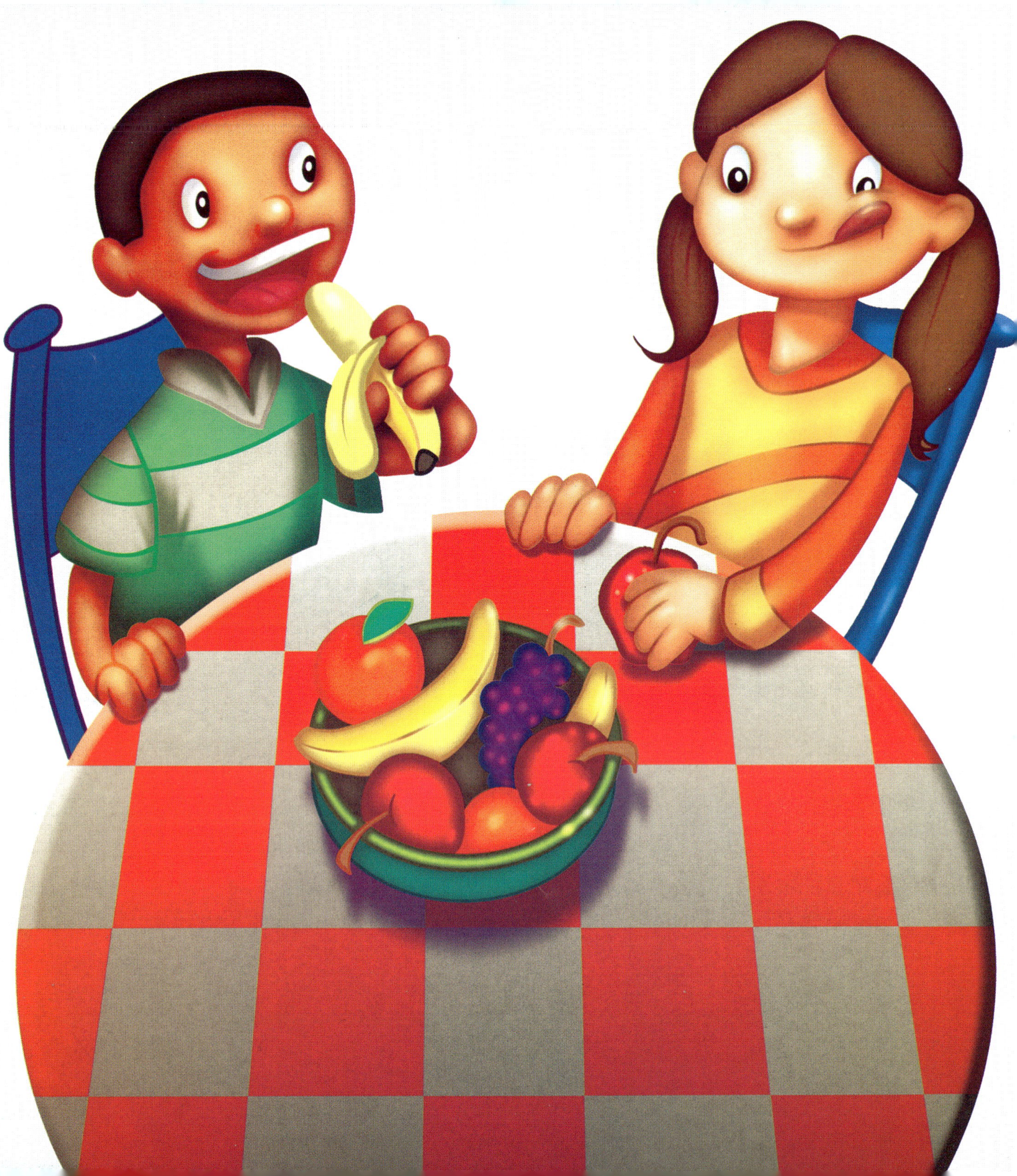

Always stay sitting at the table when you eat. Chew your food slowly and completely. Also, keep small objects out of your mouth. Toys, coins, balls, and balloons should not be chewed.

Keep plastic away from your head and face. Plastic covering your nose or mouth can make it hard for you to breathe.

14

A fire in the fireplace is warm and cozy. But a fire in your home is dangerous. Make a plan with your family for how to escape your home if there is a fire.

Choose a spot outside where you will all meet. Practice your plan. Then you'll know what to do in a real fire.

Smoke detectors "smell" smoke before you can. Their loud alarms tell you there is a fire. Your home should have one on every floor.

16

Only cords should be plugged into wall sockets. If toys or other objects are stuck into wall sockets, you could get an electric shock.

Electricity moves quickly through water. If hair dryers and other things that are plugged in fall into water, they can give you an electric shock. Keep them away from sinks or tubs.

17

Some medicine looks like candy. But medicine can make you very sick if it's not yours. Even when it's your own medicine, be sure to ask an adult for help.

Many things used in your home are poisons. Cleaning products should be used only for cleaning. Don't eat or drink anything you aren't sure about.

If a poison accidentally gets in your mouth, tell a parent right away. He or she will call a poison control center or 911 to get you help.

20

Some things at home are not for children. If you find matches or lighters, tell an adult right away. He or she can put them away so no one gets hurt.

Do your parents have guns at home? Guns should always be locked up. If you see a gun lying around, never touch it. Run and tell an adult as fast as you can.

If you call 911, don't hang up right away. The person may tell you what to do to help.

Do you know what to do if there is an emergency at home? Call 911. Explain the problem to the person on the phone. Sometimes he or she can tell where your call is coming from. But you may need to give the person your address. Knowing it will save precious time. He or she will send help to your house.

Learning these safety rules will keep you and your family safe at home.

KEY WORDS

Research has shown that as much as 65 percent of all written material published in English is made up of 300 words. These 300 words cannot be taught using pictures or learned by sounding them out. They must be recognized by sight. This book contains 121 common sight words to help young readers improve their reading fluency and comprehension. This book also teaches young readers several important content words, such as proper nouns.

Page	Sight Words First Appearance
4	a, are, at, car, do, home, like, make, or, put, things, to, together, up, what, with, you, your
5	and, be, can, few, follow, for, get, have, how, I, just, me, show, watch, will
7	always, an, ask, but, cut, even, food, help, is, it, let, not, of, out, set, should, still, take, the, use, way
9	could, don't, from, if, in, it's, keep, may, move, off, on, other, want, water, where
11	around, away, open, play, their, they, very
13	also, eat, face, hard, head, small, when
15	all, before, every, family, know, one, tell, then, there
17	give, into, only, that, them, through
18	looks, own, some
19	about, call, he, many, right, she
21	as, away, children, find, never, no, run, see, so
23	house, need, sometimes, these, time

Page	Content Words First Appearance
4	builder, dad, dolls, grilled cheese, mom, popcorn, puzzles, racer, sandwiches
5	safety rules
7	bread, knife, microwave, oven, table, vegetables
9	adult, bathroom, dinnertime, floors, kitchen, mat, path, rubber, stairs, toys, tub
11	blinds, bugs, cords, drapes, drawers, furniture, neck, shelves, windows
13	balloons, balls, coins, mouth, nose, objects, plastic
15	alarms, fire, fireplace, outside, plan, smoke detector
17	electric shock, electricity, hair dryers, sinks, wall sockets
18	candy, medicine
19	911, cleaning products, parent, poison control center, poisons
21	guns, lighters, matches
22	person
23	address, emergency, phone, problem

Check out www.av2books.com for activities, videos, audio clips, and more!

1) Go to www.av2books.com.
2) Enter book code. **AVE76454**
3) Fuel your imagination online!

www.av2books.com